Raffia Hats
and
Baskets

Raffia Hats

and
Baskets

Liz Doyle

Kangaroo Press

Acknowledgments
To Michael for patience and encouragement and to Judy for an occasional shove! And also to a bundle of talented and helpful artists and advisers.

Photography: My brother Andy Doyle of Doyle Design, Melbourne

First published in 1992 by Kangaroo Press Pty Ltd
3 Whitehall Road (P.O. Box 75) Kenthurst 2156
Typeset by G.T. Setters Pty Limited
Printed in Hong Kong by Colorcraft Ltd

ISBN 0 86417 457 8

Contents

Introduction

Essentially I am a weaver; however, weaving takes equipment and uninterrupted time. Equipment I am substantially supplied with—time is quite another issue. But all the 'mothers-who-would-be-somethings' know that story well.

So when my children were very small, I began to play with baskets and then fell into raffia. I puzzled my own way through raffia hat making and presented friends and family with my creations, often feeling a bit miffed when their enthusiasm did not match my own. It would appear that trends have now taken over and the hats are in greater demand than I can match.

So what shall I now call myself? I feel a 'Mad Hatter' would be most apt with the emphasis often falling on the adjective!

A purchased hat is a fine piece of craftswomanship if you wish to buy one, and I am kept busy supplying my hats to outlets. However I feel the real sense of satisfaction comes from creating your own unique hat with a perfect fit for you. To this end I have taught many workshops in past years and found—as I do with teaching weaving—that the enthusiasm and talent that I meet in the classes is boundless and inspiring. I enjoy meeting people through workshops and exchanging techniques, crafts and philosophies during these days.

This book is an attempt to reach those of you who cannot get to hat workshops and hopefully extend the ideas and skills of those who have already made hats.

The ideas in this book are starting points, the techniques employed are simple and versatile. Some readers will use these instructions to copy my work—many more I feel will be inspired to make their own personal designs and will easily surpass what they find in these pages.

Once you have mastered basic techniques, the fibre is yours—just play with it; it's strong, versatile and forgiving.

In my raffia travels, I have met many older folk who remember raffia well from their school days when raffia crafts were taught in schools. They are often surprised and pleased to see the resurgence of raffia crafts.

Several booklets from this era have been passed on by interested friends. One in particular is undated but at a guess would be from the late 1920s. In her introduction the author states, 'In the making

A variety of colours and shapes...

of floor covering, chair seats, hats and baskets alone there is a satisfactory little industry. At the same time, the skilled worker will find in raffia a medium for the most delicate productions. It is almost indestructible, will stand constant exposure, can be washed with impunity and dyed any colour. Added to this it is light, pleasant to handle and free from smell of any sort. Anyone taking up the work is safe to speedily recognize its charms.

'This book does not pretend to exhaust in any department the possibilities of that work, but as a guide to the beginner it comes to fill a recognized want.'

Well said, Henrietta, and so say I! I do not pretend to show the definitive art of raffia work. I am a hat maker who is sometimes inspired to play with other ideas. Here are some of them—there are many, many more.

Another booklet I have is a compendium of ideas for using viscose 'raffia' and covers all manner of useful, decorative items—an elephant-shaped bottle cover and door stop, a crocheted hair curler bag, and toilet roll covers with dolls' torsos. My, how times change! Raffia has reverted to its natural form and the crafts are simple utilitarian items again.

I hope you enjoy this book and find it useful.

The material

Raffia is stripped from under the stem of the leaves of the raffia palm which is reputedly the world's longest-leafed palm. The tree is grown in plantations in many tropical countries, in particular in eastern Africa.

The product is exported in tightly tied bundles which make the material easy to transport. I vividly remember unsheathing my first bundle of raffia and quickly finding myself enveloped in a tangled mess that just had to be worked into plaits to recreate order in my life.

It's an amazing material that's a bit untidy to work with—at least if you're a little on the chaotic side like me, but it's quick to tidy up and not at all anti-social.

I live with a large basketful in the loungeroom and a veritable nest on the studio floor at all times. I'd go so far as to say that you can trace my every movement for the last few months by my raffia 'droppings' at beaches, parks, gardens etc. I take my work everywhere with me—it's almost as transportable as knitting and it does not inhibit the conversation on which I thrive. Metres of plait can fly past over a warm teapot. So now we come to it, the Hatter does most certainly preside over far too many tea parties for her own good! Come to think of it, my problems with time may stem from my attachment to my teapot.

By the way, I'm planning a raffia tea cosy, having been prompted by a friend's memory of his great-aunt's raffia tea cosy. I'm thinking of a bee-hive shape with embroidered bees nestling around the top— and so it goes, once you start the ideas begin to flow. So now to work.

'Attacking' the bundle

Most raffia comes in bundles weighing between 1 and 2 kg—this is how you will purchase it—so you may as well plan to do a couple of articles.

As most projects require about 300 g, it is worthwhile to roughly separate your bundle into at least three smaller ones—thus cutting down on the mess factor.

When you first undo the binding thread, leave the top wrapping intact. Work just below this to separate three roughly equal bundles and tie these off separately very, very tightly. You can then unwrap the top of the bundle and tease out your three working bundles. These are now a convenient size to work with.

To begin work, put the bound end of the working bundle under your foot, select the threads that you want from the bundle and slide them out of the binding, using a bit of pressure from your foot to hold the rest still. This leaves your hands free to work.

Raffia is often fumigated before arriving in the country and methyl bromide is the recommended fumigant; the Quarantine Department, ACT, informed me that this material is not toxic to humans after being mixed with air at which time it becomes a 'something' sulphate (my memory is porous). I must confess to having done no further investigation on this matter, having been relieved to find it relatively safe. After all, I had held, rubbed, bitten and worn the material for years before I bothered to look into the matter—good news was a good place to stop wondering!

I find this a lovely material to use and as a weaver I've used lots. My hands are in excellent condition—as during my years of spinning—as the raffia has a waxy finish which rubs off. I always work with dry raffia, though others prefer to dampen it.

I was once unlucky enough to buy what was considered quite poor quality raffia. At first I was very concerned about my work, but there was nothing else available so I used it. In the process I realised that a slightly harder material has some advantages. It makes a firmer plait which is stronger and makes up into a longer-lasting hat. It is slightly harder to work with and shape into hats, but the end result is worth the effort and it's great for basketry.

Basic techniques

It is best to start off with a thinner plait to facilitate a tight spiral at the beginning of your work. Plait approx. 30 cm with 3 pieces in each strand, then build up your strands until you have the required approx. 5 strands in each for the rest of your work.

• You may need to tie your plait to something to provide some tension while you first learn to plait. As you become more proficient, you may no longer need to tension your work.
• In order to weave from left to right, if you are left handed, you will need to imagine the diagrams as reversed.
• If your plait becomes too thick and heavy, back track a bit and pull or cut out a few strands to bring it back to size. As a rule approx. 2 cm or less is an ideal width to work with.
• Always make sure that your stitching strand is strong. The temptation may be to sew with a fine thread, but this will weaken and fray, creating a weak spot in the hat which may break.
• Always join a new strand to the stitching strand with a very strong knot and test your knots by straining them. Stitch loose ends into your work to further strengthen the joins.
• When ending your work, bind off with a wrapping stitch then oversew it down to make a strong, neat finish.
• Your hat or bag is a spiral, so the place where the spiral moves from the horizontal to the vertical plane is the point at which you come closest to symmetry. If you keep all these points in line with each other, you will have a well formed, symmetrical article.

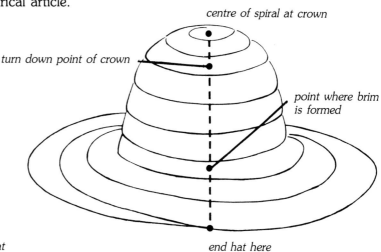

centre of spiral at crown

turn down point of crown

point where brim is formed

Making a plaited hat

end hat here

• It is best to make the crown of your hat quite deep to ensure that it stays on well; as a rule of thumb just to the top of your ears is great.
• If at any time your bag or hat becomes misshapen due to ill handling, simply press it with a hot iron and damp cloth over an appropriately shaped bowl or ball.
• Pressing is also the final ingredient to a good hat. Many uneven hats become beautiful when well pressed. Trim then press the plait before stitching, and then the hat when you have finished. Place over an appropriately shaped ball or bowl and press heavily under a wet cloth with a hot steam iron. Keep the iron moving to avoid scorching the raffia.

A very 'wonky' hat may be dunked in water and pressed.

A crown that is becoming too small during stitching can also often be dampened, pressed and stretched to its correct size—it's worth trying before you unpick and start again.

I have found raffia a very forgiving material to work with. This is not to say you need be slapdash, but many inadequacies in your work will disappear with some diligent ironing.

General instructions

Begin your work by selecting about 15-25 strands of raffia (15 for a thin starter plait). Bind off the top very tightly and tie a loop to use as a tensioning hanger. Tie this to something solid.

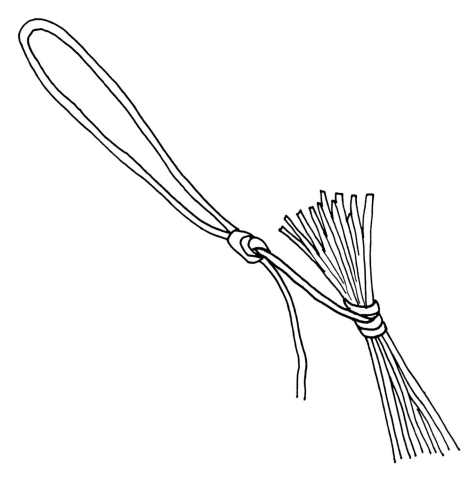

Binding off to start

3-strand plait

Divide into 3 strands and plait as for hair.

Keep your strands quite thick—you may need up to 10 pieces of raffia in each strand to achieve a plait of about 1.5 cm width. If too thin you will be plaiting and stitching forever.

If you are making a hat from your plait, be careful not to get too thick or your hat will be heavy.

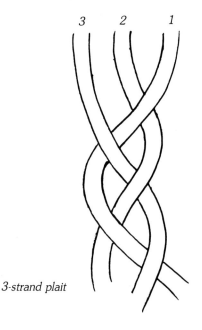

3-strand plait

4-strand plait

Divide into four strands.

Take the right-hand strand (No. 1) and cross it under No. 2, over No. 3, then No. 4 folds over No. 1.

This also can become a heavy plait. Keep your eye on the width and thickness of your bundles. Keep pressing the plait with your thumbs as you work to keep it flat.

I feel that 3 and 4 strand plaits are a bit lumpy and make better basket plaits than hats. But each to their own!

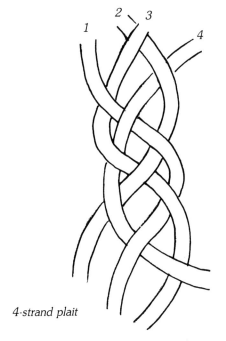

4-strand plait

5-strand plait

This is my favourite for lightweight hats and baskets. I use it 99 per cent of the time.

Divide your bundle into 5 strands and be prepared to reprogram your brain for about 1 hour. It's like learning to ride a bike or knitting. It's not really hard but requires initial concentration.

I find it useful to keep the 5 bundles separated between the fingers of my left hand for the first few plaits as there is no way to see them as separate until you get going.

Then you take the right-hand strand and weave it across—over 2, under 3, over 4 and then tuck No. 5 over it.

The right-hand strand works its way across to become strand No. 5. Pick up the new right-hand strand and weave it across again.

As you complete a pass with your weaver, pull it out and away from the work with your left hand to prevent the bottom end of the plait from tangling. Keep flattening the plait with thumb pressure as you go.

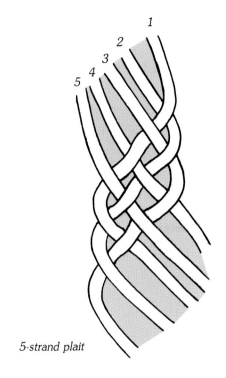

5-strand plait

Joining

Same for all plaits.

As you continue to work, you will see some pieces of raffia becoming shorter. You need to maintain a constant thickness by joining new strands in. Simply hold a new strand against your weaver. Join one new strand at a time.

At first you will feel a little clumsy introducing this new element so be a little patient.

It is easier to begin introducing a new piece when your existing strands are about 30 cm long. If you leave it too late you will have problems, as they will all get short at once. Leave the end of the new strand sticking out of your work—it can be trimmed later.

Continue on for the required length—I usually find I plait about 3 or 4 metres, then stitch, then plait again to ensure that I know when I will be finished. It would be painful to plait more than you need.

Trim off all the rough ends close to the plait.

Press the plait with a hot steam iron and damp cloth.

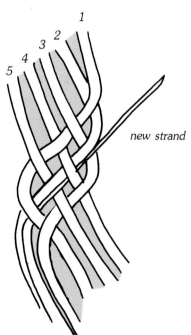

new strand

Joining in a new strand

Stitching

Twist and manipulate the start of your plait into a round or oblong spiral as required, leaving no space in the middle. The bundle at the beginning of your plait is *under* your work, so it will end up inside the hat or basket. The diagram on the next page shows the *underside* of the work.

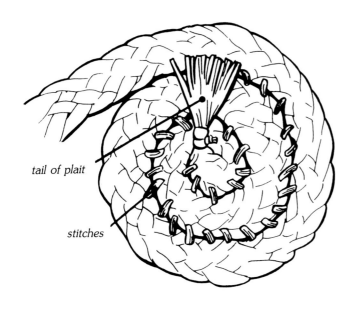

tail of plait

stitches

Stitching a round spiral, wrong side of work

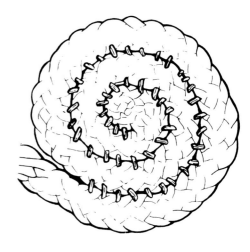

Stitching a spiral, right side

Knead and manipulate the plait into shape and prepare to stitch on the *right* side of your work.

Take a strong piece of raffia. If it's too thin, it will easily fray and weaken. Use a large-eyed tapestry or knitter's needle to stitch in a simple overhand stitch.

Make sure your stitches are close together and give each stitch a tug so that it disappears into the plait a little.

Often when you first work, you feel the stitches look obvious. Don't get too worried. The stitches are there on all hats but they become a part of the whole and pressing assists them to disappear a little. Keep them neat, small and regular and they will meld into the whole.

Shaping

The first thing I need to say about this is that I never use a block. I guess it's that thing about equipment, I would get stuck in one place with my work. Also I just don't think they're necessary. We carry a very adequate block on our shoulders.

There is very little difference in head sizes—they average 53-56 cm and sometimes 58 cm, so just ascertain where you fit in that scope, if you are making hats for others, and make the hats tight or loose as required.

To begin shaping, you should always work flat, flat, flat for the top of a crown or base of a basket.

You will need to decide whether you will begin with a round or oblong spiral. Hats that begin with an oblong spiral usually have a

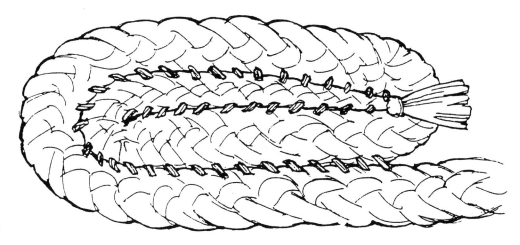

Oblong spiral, wrong side of work

3 cm oblong to begin with. I usually start with a round spiral and find these very successful.

Make the spiral flat as if you are making a table mat. Keep pressing it down with your fingers—working flat on the table will help to ensure the flatness.

Your plait will need to be gently eased or gathered to allow it to remain flat while being stitched. Keep stitching flat until the required size—see detailed directions.

There are two basic processes in shaping: gathering or easing and pulling tight or stretching the plait as you stitch.

If you ease or gather the plait, you allow the work to remain flat. If you do not gather, the work will naturally move into a gentle slope as you stitch it.

Pulling or stretching the plait as you stitch will tighten the work and cause it to pull in, for example, for creating up-turned brims.

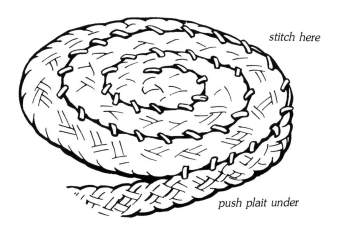

stitch here

push plait under

Creating a sharp edge by bending the plait back on itself

Bending the plait back on itself will create a sharp edge as seen on a boater hat or the edge of a basket base.

Further details of shaping for specific styles are given in the detailed instructions.

Gaily coloured raffia for a small girl's hat

Opposite page:
Keeping the sun off

Finishing the plait

It is important that you do not finish off the plait until the work is all stitched as you will not be able to achieve a symmetrical shape otherwise.

I work by plaiting, stitching, plaiting, stitching, so I can keep some degree of control about introducing colour or shaping to a finishing point. I can design as I go this way.

I prefer to be quite organic about my work and find many similarities between raffia crafts and life. If you stay open to all possibilities, you will be pleased with the result; stringent expectations may lead to disappointment. Working organically helps you to go with the compromises and meet success.

So when your work feels complete, you look for the place to finish off to achieve a well-balanced look, plait normally up to about 50 cm from this finishing point, then begin to thin the plait off by not adding new strands in or by cutting existing threads out. Work for a while, thinning the plait down gradually. As it becomes very thin, for the last 2 cm work into a 3-strand plait then bind off and stitch down neatly with an overhand stitch.

Remember a neat finish is well worth working towards.

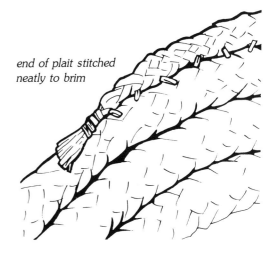

end of plait stitched neatly to brim

Finishing off by thinning the plait down

Decorations

Embroidery

Many older hats and bags were embroidered with coloured raffia. Just remember, if you choose to embroider, that your stitches are going over a rough backing so keep the ideas simple.

1. Traditional lazy daisies—like mother's old shopping basket. These are easy and effective.
2. To be a bit more adventurous, build up a colourful cottage garden on your hat. Use French knots, stem stitch and large satin stitch as your basics. Just keep going until it's done. Fill the gaps with leaves and it will look wonderful.

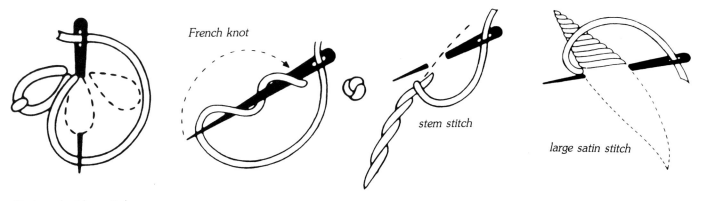

French knot

stem stitch

large satin stitch

Basic embroidery stitches

lazy daisy stitch

Flat brim hat in raffia dyed a light chestnut (page 32)

Opposite page:
Flat crowned hat with a wide brim (page 29)

Embroidering with raffia: cottage garden flowers

3. Rosebuds are lovely always.
4. Meadow daisies—use red and yellow for the flowers and surround the crown of the hat. This is very sweet for a child's hat.

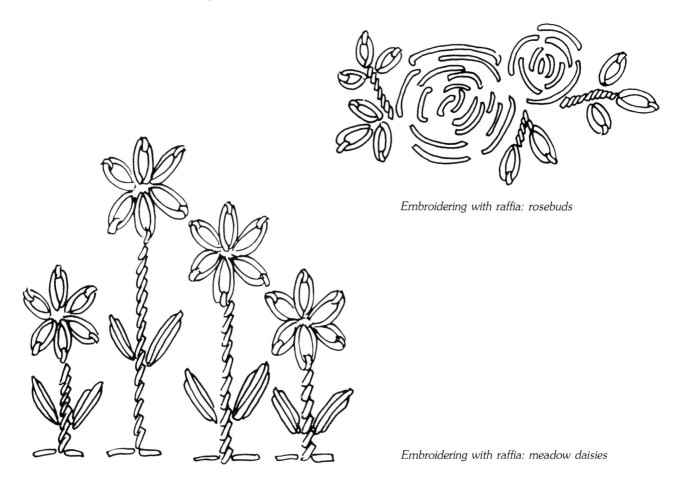

Embroidering with raffia: rosebuds

Embroidering with raffia: meadow daisies

Other forms of decoration are as diverse as you are—a hand painted or marbled silk scarf, a fat plait of coloured raffia or a simple twist of raffia with some dried flowers, a grosgrain ribbon, georgette flowers—you name it.

I tend to go simple with my hats and make the trim loose so it can be swapped around to match my outfits.

Woven decoration

It is really lovely and individual to weave colour into your plait. This can be done at random throughout the whole hat, just grabbing a coloured strand to add to bundles, or in specific places. You must sew the hat closely after each section of plaiting to be able to introduce a stripe of colour at the correct part of the hat.

Dyeing

Raffia takes dye excellently; both vegetable and chemical dyes can be used successfully.

I have used fibre-reactive dyes for cotton and wool and acid milling dyes successfully.

I find that best results are obtained in a hot dye bath. I loosen the tight binding on the skein and tie it loosely in several places. I then wet it thoroughly and submerge in the hot dye bath. The raffia will be dyed after 10 minutes of simmering or soaking (in very hot water). It can then be rinsed and dried thoroughly.

You will find that the dye bath can be used several times giving lighter shades, or mix with another colour for variety of hues.

Hat with sharply upturned brim (page 33) trimmed with a loose heavy plait of raffia

Half profile brim style, created by pulling tightly on one or two rows in one part of the brim (page 34)

Hats

These instructions will take you through the various elements of individual hats, for example, round or flat crown, flat, rolled or partially turned brim. You can select the elements you need to make your own style, or copy one of those in the photographs.

You can weave one or many coloured strands into your hat as you go to make it individual.

• *Materials.* All hats weigh less than 300 g (or we'd all have bent necks).

• Remember to use the general instructions (pages 13- 20) for plaiting and stitching techniques.

Hat with rounded crown

I do not ever use a hat block to stitch my hats, but if you have one available, try it and find out what you think. Wooden blocks are truly beautiful things.

Stitch a flat spiral of approx. 7.5 cm diameter. Watch for an approximation of symmetry, then gently slope the sides as you stitch—this is achieved by stopping the easing process and also leaning the plait over slightly. Keep trying the hat on in front of a mirror as you work. Loosely follow the round of your crown. Don't make it too tight; if it is becoming tight, dampen, stretch, then iron—this will stretch it. One extreme case occurred in a workshop, where a woman had worked diligently to get a half crown that was more than a little tight. I put the wet cloth and iron flat down onto the top of the crown and ironed it almost flat—it worked remarkably well. So try this if your work is getting small.

It is best to make the crown quite deep—the tip of the ears or below is best.

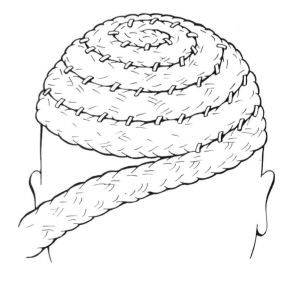

work carefully around the head

Making a rounded crown

Hat with flat crown

Work a flat spiral to the width of your head. Work until symmetrical then turn the plait back on its underside and stitch for one round while you hold in this position.

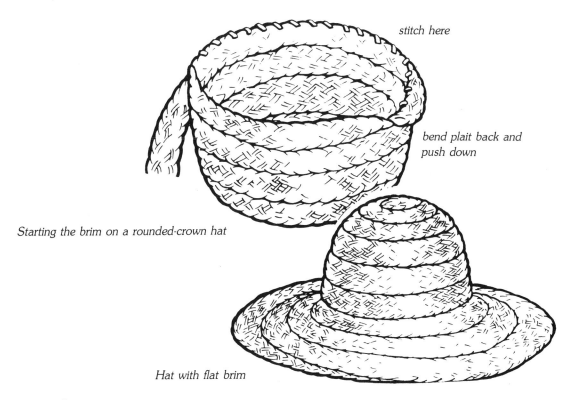

stitch here

bend plait back and push down

Starting the brim on a rounded-crown hat

Hat with flat brim

Now stitch around vertically trying on as you go—you may need to ease the plait slightly to enlarge it a little as you go, or conversely tighten it a little. If these movements are made gradually, you will get a nice line and good fit.

29

Above:
Sou'wester, created by rolling up most of the brim using the half profile technique (page 34)

Opposite page:
A slightly more exaggerated half profile brim than the one shown on page 27

Brim styles

At this stage you begin to stitch under the brim. Turning out for the brim has two options. Again look for the point of symmetry—I find this easy on a flat-topped hat as you find the place where the plait moved from the horizontal to the vertical plane. A round crown is more difficult. I usually count the rounds in several places around the hat to find this spot.

The first option will give a smooth curve onto the brim; this is achieved by turning the plait on a right angle to the crown—the weight of the brim will cause this to bend out in a smooth curve.

By folding the plait completely back against the outside of the crown and stitching one round in that position, you will achieve a much sharper turn, as for a boater.

There are four main brim styles. All start with flat work as for the beginning of the crown: ease the plait; work on a flat surface if necessary to maintain a good flat brim. Do not ease the plait too much as this creates a floppy brim.

Flat brim
Take the brim completely out flat if you require this style—don't make the brim too narrow, 4 rounds minimum.

Rolled-up brim
This is created by making at least 3 rounds flat then a stretched round. Stretch quite strongly but not too tight—this may take trial and error. Another round added to this will create a deeper upturn.

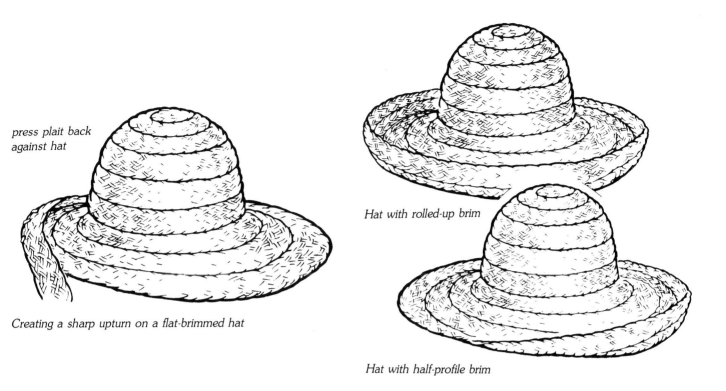

press plait back against hat

Creating a sharp upturn on a flat-brimmed hat

Hat with rolled-up brim

Hat with half-profile brim

Sharp upturn

You can also create a flat-brimmed hat with one row of sharp upturn to give a stylish hat—this will also hold a floppy hat brim into a tight flat style. This style is particularly popular with older women.

Half profile

By pulling the final one or two rows tightly in one part of the brim you will create my favourite style. I have made many variations on it and found it always exciting. The hat can be designed to be worn in any direction to suit the mood. I call these my 'impressionist' hats.

Sou'wester

This technique can also be used to create the sou'wester style, which is also appealing and popular. More of the brim is rolled up for this style.

This is my latest favourite and suits younger women beautifully.

Brim styles are open to your creative impulse, and again I stress that the major attraction of making your own hat is your ability to find the style that suits you best.

All my hats suit me—I can't help it!

Basketry

Raffia is strong, soft and supple and takes no preparation; it is an excellent material for beginning basketry techniques. It makes strong and serviceable baskets which can be used for utility tasks.

My baskets here tend towards simplicity as they are intended to appeal to beginners to 'have a go' and then move on to their own designs. I have used 3-strand and 5-strand plaits and a simple coiling technique to indicate the potential of raffia for simple basketry.

Of course there are many other variations of these techniques which are open to being used with raffia. A 7-strand plait stitched to a wooden base makes a great shopping basket, twined raffia over a cane framework is lovely, a plait can be woven in and out on a cane framework.

Once you have gained the basic techniques for handling and shaping the material, the options are as vast as your imagination. The classic sewing basket, a pincushion with a sand-filled cloth bag inserted into a small basket, children's slippers and a variety of tableware, as well as serviceable storage baskets, are all possibilities for this material.

I have also recently seen a beautiful carry basket for a doll handmade by a friend, which opens up the potential of the material for accessories for dolls.

The techniques I have used for any of these baskets are interchangeable—for example, you could use a 3-strand plait to make a carry bag. Therefore you can choose any shape and any technique and swap them around to create your own piece.

The hat on the left has a flat crown and wide flat brim. The sou'wester on the right has a gently rolled brim

Baskets in a variety of shapes

Small carry basket

This is a very simple and serviceable bag which of course can be embellished with the addition of coloured raffia as used in the large basket or with coloured stitching and embroidery.

When I first began making hats, I immediately recalled a childhood memory of walking beside my mother's raffia basket, plastic lined and embroidered with lazy daisies. This is the inspiration for this bag, with longer handles for shoulder straps. I couldn't come at the flowers!

Materials
500 g raffia

Method
Make a 5-strand plait of approx. 3 cm width. Begin stitching by creating a 15 cm long oval. (See diagram.)

Continue the base in this oblong shape until it measures approx. 35 cm by 20 cm.

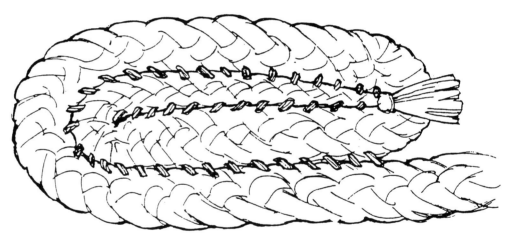

Make a sharp turn up the sides by folding the plait back onto itself for one round; begin this turn at one end of the oval.

Continue up the sides, easing the plait slightly as you go around the ends of the oval to create a gentle outwards slope on the ends, while maintaining flat sides. The sides should be about 25 cm high.

Thin your plait down until it finishes off at the same end as the one you began turning up for the sides. Tuck the final end of the plait inside the basket and stitch down.

Make 3 more lengths of plait all approx. 100 cm long.

Two of these are stitched firmly into place on each side of the basket to form handles, and the third is stitched around inside the top edge of the basket to strengthen the edge and to reinforce the handle joins.

This last plait is strongly overstitched along the top edge of the basket with several strong stitches through the handles, basket and lining plait to further strengthen the handles. This point will carry all the weight of the basket and will be the first place to wear out. So make it really strong.

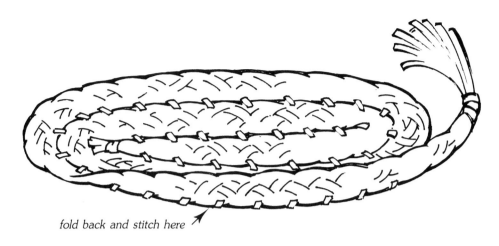

fold back and stitch here ↗

Small carry basket: starting the sides

This is a good place to add embellishment if you want to as it will again help to strengthen this point.

The length of plait stitched inside the neck of the basket not only acts as reinforcement but also as a trim to cover the top of a lining if you wish to line your basket.

The ever-useful small
carry basket
(page 38)

A capacious handbag (page 42)

Handbag

This is a very serviceable small basket that can be used as a handbag. It's a good basic shape and could be developed to suit your needs— for example, an oval stitched to one side of the top to form a flap, or a different handle, would make it your own design.

I found when I first made this basket that it looked rather bland with a straight handle joined on each side, so I took the handle off and broke it into finer plaits to create some balance and detail.

The clasp on this bag is made of a lovely piece of driftwood which is easily available to me by the beach, but a knot of wood, a shell or a button would make it your own; or you could make a raffia knot or button—it's up to you.

Materials
300 g raffia

Method
Begin with an oval base and work until it measures 18 cm × 14 cm. (See instructions for small carry basket.)

Start the turn up for the sides at one end of the oval. Turn the plait back on itself by bending it onto the inside of the basket for one round and overstitching.

Work around the oval, moving the shape out gently as you go; ease more on the end of the oval but also slightly on the side. Keep going up and out until the sides are 15 cm high. At this point the work should measure approx. 85 cm around.

Bend the plait over 90 degrees to stitch the next round, thus forming the angle before shaping the bag inwards for the neck.

Continue stitching, moving the shape in by slightly stretching the plait as you go for 3 more rounds.

Taper the plait to finish off at the end of the oval, in line with the point at which you first turned up for the side, to create symmetry.

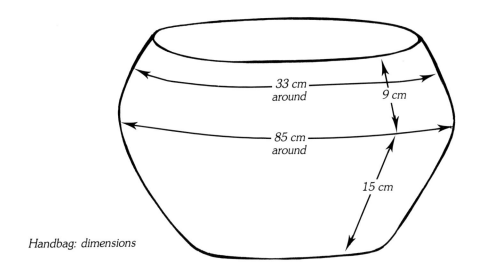

Handbag: dimensions

33 cm
around

9 cm

85 cm
around

15 cm

The strap is 160 cm long—80 cm of this is a thin, strong 5-strand plait, very tightly plaited; the rest is left unplaited to start with, 40 cm at each end. This is done by tightly binding the bundle 40 cm from the start, then plaiting for 80 cm. Now separate the strands into 2 or 3 bundles according to your preference and plait each bundle into a 3-strand plait, working tightly.

Go back to where you bound off to begin the 5-strand plait, undo the binding and separate into 2 or 3 bundles (this need not match the other end of the handle if you prefer the bag to be asymmetrical).

Bind each plait off tightly and pin into position on the bag with dressmaker's pins—the only rule here is to check that the bag hangs well and is comfortable for wearing, otherwise where you position the handle is your own design decision.

Beach basket
trimmed with a stripe
of coloured raffia
(page 46)

44

Chunky small storage basket with lid (page 48)

Once you have found the compromise between design, balance and function, you can stitch the plaits into position on the bag by stitching through the plaiting and the bag with a strong thread. Try to make your stitches follow the strands of the plait, so they disappear as you work. Remember, the more stitching, the greater the strength, so be generous.

Twist the very ends of these thin plaits into a tight spiral to stitch down and create a neat finish *or* you can push them through the plait of the basket and knot them off on the inside so that they disappear completely.

The clasp. Stitch a shell, button, buckle, piece of driftwood or whatever onto the basket halfway along the top on one side. This can be put anywhere on the basket to suit your own design. I positioned my driftwood 'button' halfway along the 3rd round of the plait from the top.

On the other side I stitched a small 3-strand plait in two places to create a loop which slips over the button. This small plait measures 25 cm.

It may be interesting to plait the handle and button loop in dyed raffia, or make the whole basket in dyed raffia. This is of course always an option with all the hats and baskets.

Beach basket

Materials
600 g raffia

Method
The beach basket is a larger project, taking more time but no more skill than a hat. It complements a raffia hat and is a strong and useful basket for the beach, shopping or everyday use. I love this basket and use it continuously. It is capacious and convenient.

Plaiting. The plait used for making this basket should be strong and slightly thicker than a hat plait. There are approximately 15 metres of plaiting in this basket so you'll be an expert plaiter by the time you finish this project; but that's okay, the basket will be beautiful!

Shaping the basket base. Form your plait into an oblong approx. 30 cm long and stitch around it until the base measures approx. 40 cm × 12 cm.

The sides of the basket. Turn the plait back on itself and begin to stitch on the outside of the bag. You will now find that you have a 90 degree turn between the base and side of the basket. It is best to start this turn up on one end of the oval and call that your starting and finishing place for each round to help you achieve symmetry.

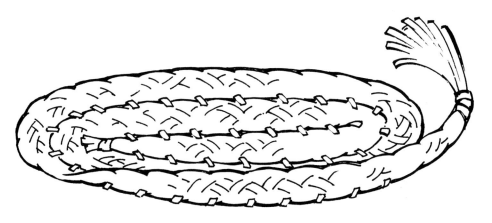

As the basket progresses up the sides, you need to ease the plait slightly as you stitch around each end. This will cause the shape to extend out slowly at each end while the sides remain flat. Do this shaping carefully, keeping an eye on the way it goes to make sure each end is the same. Make 6 rounds.

The coloured stripe. Begin joining coloured raffia into your plait as you run out. You just use a few strands of colour, or slowly make the plait totally coloured for a few metres, then go back to natural. This is your decision, to make your bag unique. Just remember to start and finish the coloured areas at the point of symmetry on your basket. Do two rounds of colour. At this point, the basket is 20 cm high and 125 cm around.

Shaping the top. When you have completed stitching 8 rounds up the sides you need to start shaping the bag in slightly to create the neck. Do this by gently tightening the plait as you stitch at the two ends.

Finishing the shape. Continue shaping the bag for one more round of natural, then 2 rounds of coloured, then begin thinning your plait down for the last 30 cm until it is finally thin enough to bind off at the point of symmetry. The neck should measure about 105 cm when finished.

The handle. Plait 3 metres of finer strong plait. Also make 4 small 3-strand plaits 5 cm long to use as tabs for the handle inside the basket. (See diagram.) Now go back to the points on the basket marked in the diagram and cut your stitching to form a slit approx. 2.5 cm wide for the handle to slip through. Carefully overstitch each side of the slit to strengthen your stitching.

Attach a small plait at the 4 positions marked on the diagram with a firm overhand stitch and thread the handle plait through the slits and tabs.

Stitch the two ends of the handle together and to the base of the basket *very firmly*. This is the weakest point of the bag: make sure it's done well!

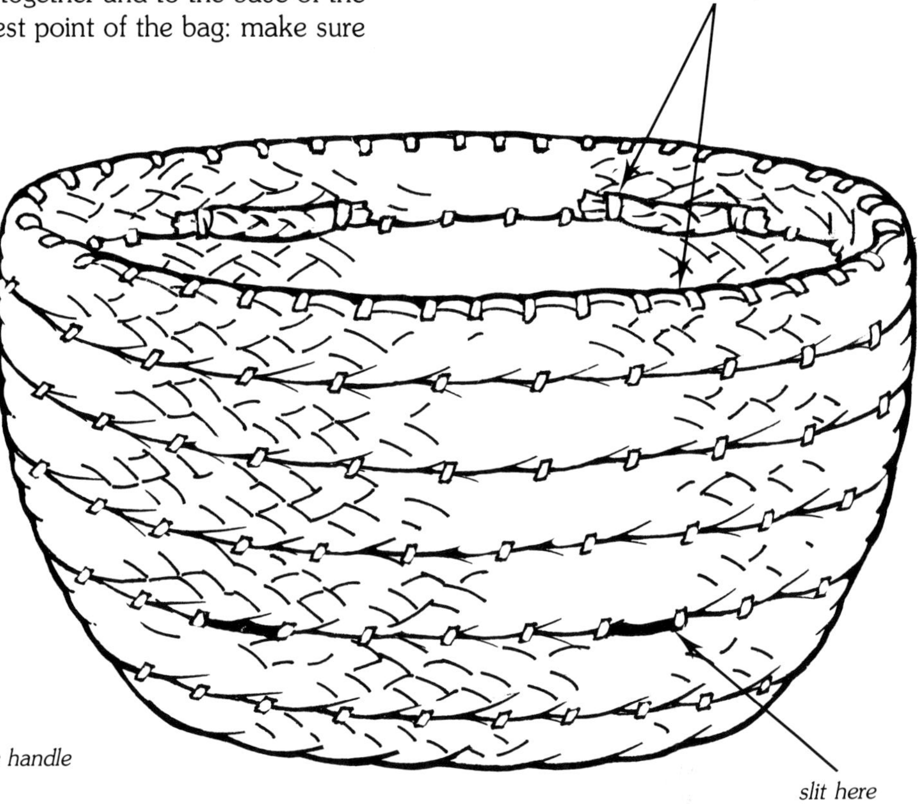

affix strips

slit here

Beach basket: attaching the handle

Small storage basket with lid

I felt that the 3-strand plait would make an interesting beehive design— well I didn't really achieve it this time but I'm working on it.

As this plait is rougher and lumpier than the 5-strand it makes a nice little 'lumpy' affair and has excellent potential for creating very large baskets for storage. I can see this one growing into a tall laundry basket one day soon. This plait also has potential for making a sewing basket if you're not too good at coiling.

Materials
500 g raffia

Method
Remember to keep your plait fat with approx. 12 pieces per strand. It should remain about 2 cm wide.

Stitch into a round spiral to start and work flat until the base measures approx. 25 cm.

Turn up for the sides with a 90 degree bend to create a smooth turn and work a vertical cylinder for approx. 15 cm or as you require (this basket would be very cute if it was squat). On the final round, stretch the plait quite firmly as you stitch to cause the neck of the basket to draw in.

Taper the plait down, causing it to finish in a position that creates symmetry, and bind off tightly and stitch down.

Now begin a new plait and again begin stitching in a round spiral. Stay flat for at least 5 cm then gently slope the work down and out by not easing the plait too much as you stitch. This will cause a 45 degree slope to occur. Work until the lid is as wide as the neck of the basket. Make the last round vertical by holding the plait at a 90 degree angle to the rest of the work while stitching: this will create a gentle bend in the finished piece. Taper the plait off to create a symmetrical lid.

I then went about looking for the right handle which I found in my convenient tray of 'beach finds'. You must now find your own special piece to finish the basket.

A posy of embroidered flowers on the top would give the basket a totally different feel from my slightly Japanese version.

A collection of Aboriginal baskets

Opposite page:
This dilly basket crammed with shells is based on an Aboriginal design
(page 52)

Small dilly basket

I based this baby basket on a small Aboriginal basket that I really love. it is very easy and so small it takes no time at all.

Materials
150 g plain raffia
50 g coloured raffia

Method
Make a 5-strand plait of approx. 3 metres and stitch into a round spiral approx. 20 cm in diameter. Turn up for the sides by folding the plait back on itself, wrong sides together as you stitch one round. Now take the sides up vertically for 3 rounds. Begin introducing colour into the plait as it ends the third round and work enough coloured plait to complete one round. Stitch in place, tapering the plait so it finishes off to make the cylinder symmetrical.

Plait a coloured 3-strand plait for the handle, approx. 50 cm long, and stitch securely into place. I twisted the end of this plait into a spiral and rosette to be stitched down as some detail.

This is a cute little basket for a small girl to use. It could be worked plain with ribbons and flowers to decorate it. As a household decoration, it can be filled with shells, flowers or potpourri, and it could certainly have several bigger or smaller sisters.

This basket should not, however, be made too large as it will not hold shape when carrying weight. It would be necessary to purchase a wooden basket base of the correct size and stitch the plait for the sides of the basket to it to carry weight.

Coiled baskets

Coiling can be a slow technique when employed with full wrapping as in the Gumnut basket shown in this section, or faster work if done over an exposed core as shown in the darning basket. This technique can be used with many materials, either found or purchased. Raffia is a fabulous material to practise the technique with as it is strong and easily manipulated.

I have found coiling a wonderful way to use up raffia which is too woody to use for plaiting.

I also really love the finesse of the finished articles as the coil can be manipulated with far greater detail to achieve finer shapes than can be achieved with plaiting. There are several coiling techniques and the Aboriginal baskets shown in the plate exhibit the potential of this type of work and the possibilities for using colour as you work.

I can recall being really inspired by the potential of coiled baskets when I first saw a Yugoslavian bread-rising basket—the core was of straw about 4 cm in diameter and was stitched with rough string. The basket was approx. 50 cm high and wide. It was designed with a lid to hold the bowl of rising dough and provide insulation. It was so rough and functional.

Gumnut trimmed basket is made by the wrapped coil technique

Gumnut basket

Materials
300 g raffia

Method
Take approx. 20 strands of strong raffia. Bind off very tightly and shape into a tight spiral. Keep the binding thread in the needle and use this to wrap around the core neatly until you have done one round, then stitch the next round of the core to the first. Wrap the core 3 times then stitch back over the first round—wrap 3 times, stitch once below.

Position the holding stitches in a radiating spiral as you work. This will mean wrapping 4 times in the next round, 5 in the next, then 6 times. The next time, you will make a new holding stitch after the 3rd wrap, creating a new line of stitches and closing up what is becoming an ever-widening gap.

New stitching material can be joined by tightly knotting the new to the old in such a way that the knot disappears into the area between the two coils.

New coil material is held onto the coil as it is being wrapped.

It is best to work in a spiral that leaves the unused part of the coil easily held in your non-dominant hand; the illustrations here show the best direction for a right-handed worker, left-handed workers turn the other way.

Make the flat base approx. 10 cm diameter then begin to shape up the sides by positioning the coil slightly on top of the last coil and keep stitching.

Shape the basket out gently until the sides are approx. 7–8 cm high, then begin shaping in to make a smooth curve. Be patient and

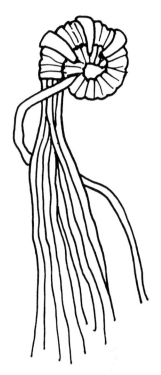

Coiled work: starting a spiral

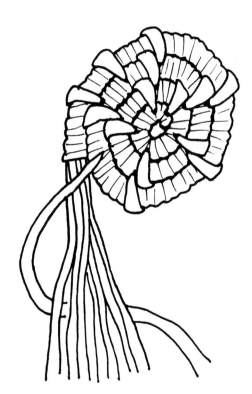

Coiled work: pattern of holding stitches

watch the shape as you go—sometimes a cardboard template can help you to keep the shape correct around the basket.

Work inwards, flattening out the curve until you have a neck of approx. 7 cm diameter. Thin the coil down slowly until you can see a symmetrical circle and fasten off by overstitching into place.

Lid. Begin a new spiral, and work out in a curve that complements the basket until you overlap the opening by 2 cm. Then fasten down the core and overstitch the end neatly.

Now begin the last coil and stitch it into place under the lid inside the 2 cm mark. This will create a lip that will fit into the basket. Wrap and stitch onto the underside of the lid, and continue in a vertical position for about 3 rounds or until the lip will hold the lid in place. Taper off the core and overstitch the ends into place. Decorate the top.

Coiled darning basket with exposed core

Grandma had one for holding the socks and darning equipment.

This basket is slightly rougher than the fully-wrapped Gumnut basket and therefore faster to do. The coil can be as thick as you wish and can be stitched with raffia, linen thread or waxed thread.

The core material or the stitching material can be coloured as both show up in the work.

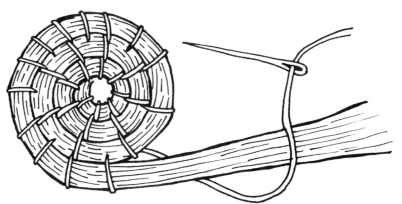

Coiled work: spiral with exposed core

Method
Bind off the core bundle tightly, and make the first spiral turn, completely wrapping this time to create a neat beginning. (See diagram.)

This basket is stitched in the very simple spiral stitch. There are many other ways to stitch over an exposed core and these are expertly handled in *Fibre Basketry Homegrown and Hand Made*, edited by Helen Richardson (Kangaroo Press).

Stitch through the previous round from the front of your work, pull around to the front again, position the stitch with your fingers then

start the next stitch. Pull tight when in position. Make a stitch approximately every 1 cm and keep these stitches radiating neatly. As the work progresses stitches will become more widely spaced and an additional stitch will need to be placed between each stitch of the previous round—I suggest the maximum gap between stitches should be approx. 1 cm.

Continue working in a flat spiral until the base measures approx. 30 cm, then position the next coil slightly on top of the last to begin building up the sides. Shape the sides as you want them as you go, watching carefully for symmetry. Stand back often.

Work outwards until the sides measure 10 cm high, then begin curving them in until the mouth has a diameter of 20 cm. Thin the core down to create symmetry and overstitch for 2 cm on the end.

Lid. Begin a new coil and stitch into a flat smooth curve until it is 2 cm wider than the hole in the neck of the basket. Now edge the coil back in as you work until it is small enough to fit back into the neck of the basket, then work vertically for two rounds to create the lip on the lid.

Insert colour into your coil as you require for your design.

I have made a miniature coil for the knob on this basket and stitched it on firmly. You may choose a natural article (shell, knot of wood or seed). Make sure you stitch this on firmly.

Flower basket

This is simple simple simple! It is one large, flat circle held up by the 'ricrac' handles.

Materials
300 g plain raffia
2 pieces of dried willow or fine cane, approximately 1 metre long

Coiled darning basket made by the exposed core technique (page 56); below is a detail of the coiled lid

58

The wonderfully simple flower trug (page 57)

Method

Work a 5-strand plait and stitch into a flat circle until approx. 50 cm diameter. Thin the plait down and finish off for a symmetrical effect. Bind and stitch down.

Now plait a 5-strand plait using 4 strands of raffia bundles and the soaked willow or cane as the 5th strand. (See diagram.) You will find that the willow/cane strand does not bend, so the raffia plait 'ricracs' around it.

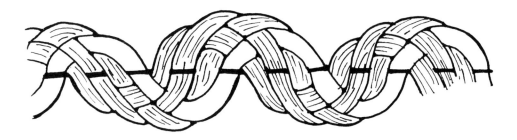

Flower basket: the handle

This is decorative, but more importantly it strengthens the handles so they remain rigid and cause the sides of the basket to roll up into that lovely flower-trug shape.

Now position the handles under two opposite sides of the basket, over-lapping the neatened off ends, and stitch them into place right along the points where the handle makes contact with the basket.

Position the handles so that they lean towards the centre of the basket and stitch them together in two places at the top.

Decorate your basket with embroidered flowers or stitch dried flowers into place on one side.

Suppliers

RAFFIA

Liz Doyle
Bulk raffia, coloured raffia and ready-made
plaiting
Cnr Bay & Tathra Sts
Tathra NSW 2550
(064) 94-1401

Raffial
(Wholesale or mail order)
P.O. Box 124
Tathra NSW 2550

Easy Craft
(Wholesale)
56 Hotham Rd
Artarmon NSW 2064
(02) 438-5448

Mr Craft
Coolgun Lane
Eastwood NSW 2122
(02) 858-2868

Art Mat
21 Queens Ave
Hawthorn Vic 3122
(03) 819 2133

Wondoflex
1353 Malvern Rd
Malvern Vic 3144
(03) 822-6231

DYES

Gay Wool Dyes
(Most good craft outlets)

Rhonda Trounce Raffia Dyes
77 Bluebell Drive
Wamberal NSW 2260
(043) 84-2288

Index